A souvenir guide

# Beatrix Potter's Hill Top
## Cumbria

Claire Masset

**National Trust**

# Hill Top, Beatrix Potter's Paradise

'My purchase seems to be regarded as a huge joke; I have been going over my hill with a tape measure,' Beatrix Potter wrote to her publisher, Frederick Warne, in October 1905.

That summer Beatrix had acquired Hill Top, a working farm in the village of Near Sawrey, and was looking forward to making it her own. She was an unlikely buyer. What did a single, middle-aged woman from London, with no knowledge of farming and a blossoming career in publishing, want with a farm in the Lake District?

Hill Top, it turned out, was one of many purchases Beatrix made in the area, but this was the one she would treasure the most. 'In her eyes it was more than just a little farmhouse in the Lake District – it was her symbol of freedom,' wrote Beatrix Potter's first biographer, Margaret Lane. By acquiring Hill Top, Beatrix, aged 39, was able to escape the shackles of her formal London upbringing and carve out a new life for herself – one in tune with her need for simplicity and escape, nature and inspiration.

Beatrix filled Hill Top with mementoes and antiques, local furniture and favourite paintings, until it became a personal museum. She created a garden that reflected her love of the informal and rustic and which inspired many of her illustrations, as did her house.

Hill Top is now a shrine to Beatrix Potter, each room imbued with her spirit. It is the closest you will ever get to this extraordinary woman. To walk the path she trod every day, to witness the frothy charm of her cottage garden, to be enveloped by the cosy atmosphere of the Entrance Hall and pore over her treasured possessions in each of its six rooms, is to get a sense of Beatrix's complex character. For though she is best remembered for creating Peter Rabbit and other much-loved children's characters, Beatrix Potter wasn't just a talented writer and illustrator. She was a shrewd businesswoman, a self-taught botanist, a farmer, a vital supporter of the National Trust, one of the most passionate and successful conservationists of her time and, perhaps most importantly in her eyes, a wife.

Left The view of Hill Top from above the Orchard

Right Beatrix at Hill Top in her later years

# An Extraordinary Woman

Beatrix Potter (1866–1943) is famous throughout the world for her 'little books'. Still today, over 100 years after *The Tale of Peter Rabbit* was published in 1902, the naughty little rabbit in the blue jacket is one of the most loved children's characters.

What is surprising is that Beatrix's life didn't actually revolve around the 23 books she wrote and illustrated, and which were hugely successful in her lifetime. In 1925, when the editor of the American magazine *The Horn* asked Beatrix to describe herself, she wrote: 'Beatrix Potter is Mrs William Heelis. She lives in the north of England, her home is amongst the mountains and lakes that she has drawn in her picture books. Her husband is a lawyer. They have no family. Mrs Heelis is in her 60th year. She leads a very contented life, living always in the country and managing a large sheep farm on her own land… I don't think anybody requires to know more about me.'

Beatrix disliked publicity. But this description also shows that she didn't just want to be known as a successful author-illustrator, but as a wife and a farmer. 'I hold an old-fashioned notion that a happy marriage is the crown of a woman's life,' she once stated. Unlike her contemporary Virginia Woolf, Beatrix was not a feminist. She did, however, break the boundaries of what a Victorian woman was meant to do in life, pursuing her interests with passion, unconcerned with what people might think.

Beatrix used the money she earned from her books to buy farms and land that were under threat of development. She became an expert farmer and a passionate conservationist, working closely with the National Trust to help preserve Lake District land.

Beatrix Potter is a fascinating contradiction. Although fiercely independent, she remained a dutiful daughter and, after her marriage, insisted on being called Mrs Heelis. Her illustrations have a nostalgic, fairy-tale quality to them, yet the stories themselves are firmly rooted in reality: ducks are chased by foxes, rabbits are hunted by cats and threatened by gardeners… Beatrix had no children of her own but was able to communicate with them in a unique way. She liked to say that she could see fairies, yet she was also entirely pragmatic and unpretentious. In her later years, anyone who suggested that her painting was 'art' would be told: 'Great rubbish, absolute bosh!'

'I never quite understood the secret of Peter's perennial charm. Perhaps it is because he and his little friends keep on their way, busily absorbed in their own doings.'

### A secret diary
Between the ages of 14 and 30 Beatrix kept a journal written in code. The code involved the simple substitution of a letter for another letter or symbol, yet it remained a mystery until 1958, when Beatrix Potter expert and collector, Leslie Linder, finally deciphered it. The journal shows Beatrix to be a witty young woman with a natural curiosity for nature and the arts.

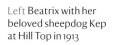

Left Beatrix with her beloved sheepdog Kep at Hill Top in 1913

# A lonely childhood

**Like many Victorian middle-class children Beatrix Potter led a secluded childhood. Looked after by a series of nurses and governesses, she spent much of her youth in the nursery at 2 Bolton Gardens, South Kensington.**

## Bolton Gardens

Born on 28 July 1866, Beatrix Potter was the elder child and only daughter of Rupert William Potter and Helen Leech. Both her parents came from wealthy cotton merchant families. Rupert, although trained as a lawyer, had little need to practise. Theirs was the life of a leisured, well-to-do family. Helen, a somewhat distant mother, filled her days with a strict routine of social engagements. Her father, more attentive to his daughter, spent his time discussing art, politics and literature with friends, visiting exhibitions, and indulging his passion for photography. Their house was typically Victorian. Dark, stuffy and oppressive, Beatrix hated it. She later called it her 'unloved birthplace'.

## A room of her own

Lacking friends for company, Beatrix created a fantasy world in the seclusion of her nursery. Delicate and often ill, she turned to drawing and painting for comfort. Both her parents were amateur artists and encouraged Beatrix in her hobby, allowing her to spend hours studying and recording nature. Nothing was too small for her gaze. Spider, ladybird, bat or lizard, the young Beatrix approached her subjects with the attention of a naturalist and the hand of an artist.

**Above** Beatrix aged five at Dalguise House

**Left** View from the Potters' house at Bolton Gardens, photographed by Rupert Potter in 1889

## Getting away from London

Frequent trips to the countryside offered the children glimpses of freedom. Beatrix's paternal grandparents, Edmund and Jessie Potter, lived at Camfield Place in Hertfordshire, a large country house which the family often visited at weekends.

Every April, the family went on a two- or three-week holiday to the seaside while the London home was spring cleaned, but it was the summer holidays that provided a prolonged escape. For three months the Potters rented a house in a suitably picturesque setting. Between the ages of five and 15, Beatrix spent every summer at Dalguise House, a large mansion near Dunkeld in Perthshire. It was here that she truly fell in love with the natural world.

## Strange menagerie

Beatrix's only regular companion was her younger brother Bertram, who shared her love of art and nature. Together they collected insects and smuggled live animals into the nursery. Gradually they amassed a curious collection: a frog called Punch, two lizards called Toby and Judy, a dormouse named Xarifa, a family of snails, mice, newts, a ring snake, salamanders, a bat, a tortoise and a hedgehog called Tiggy. Beatrix also acquired a rabbit, Benjamin H. Bouncer, the original Benjamin Bunny. He was followed by Peter Piper, who became the model for Peter Rabbit. These were not only much-loved pets but creatures to be meticulously observed, their daily habits fastidiously recorded in notebooks.

'Thank goodness I was never sent to school; it would have rubbed off some of the originality.'

# Art and inspiration

**Although nature was her main inspiration, Beatrix had a lively imagination. 'The whole countryside belonged to the fairies,' she wrote. Her art became, as her biographer Margaret Lane described it, 'a delicate blend of nature and fantasy'.**

## Stories and pictures

Books and stories captured Beatrix's imagination. As a young girl she would listen with delight to the tales her grandmother Jessie told her. She was a keen reader, too. Aged six or seven, she acquired a copy of *Alice's Adventures in Wonderland* and became fascinated by the illustrations, relishing the same attention on picture books as she did on nature. As she grew up Beatrix was able to see art first hand, when she accompanied her father to Royal Academy exhibitions and London galleries. Noting her impressions in her journal, she developed a keen eye for aesthetics.

'It is all the same, drawing, painting, modelling, the irresistible desire to copy any beautiful object which strikes the eye. Why cannot I be content to look at it? I cannot rest, I must draw, however poor the result, and when I have a bad time come over me it is a stronger desire than ever.'

Right Beatrix Potter aged 17 photographed by her father in 1883 accompanied by the family spaniel, Spot

Beatrix's desire to understand nature was so strong that she was not past skinning a dead animal to understand how its body worked, or boiling it down to study its skeleton. This in-depth knowledge allowed her to produce paintings that capture the nature of an animal so that, even when it is drawn fully clothed and humanised, it retains a truthfulness that is uniquely appealing. After having been generous with advice on mixing paint, family friend John Everett Millais told Beatrix: 'Many people can see, but you have observation.'

## Fungi fascination

'Of all the hopeless things to draw, I should think the very worst is a fine fat fungus.' Between 1880 and 1901, Beatrix produced over 300 botanical drawings of fungi. She became so obsessed with the subject that she started cultivating spores and even wrote a paper entitled 'On the Germination of Spores of Agaricineae', which was presented at the Linnean Society of London on 1 April 1897. Despite her research not being acknowledged by the academic world (no doubt because she was a woman), her illustrations of fungi are so accurate that they are still used in textbooks today.

Above **Sketches of blue tits**

## A naturalist's obsession

Beatrix worked tirelessly. Every object or animal she acquired she drew, filling little books with studies of birds' eggs, butterflies, flowers, insects and fossils. She created exquisitely detailed watercolours of her pets showing them from different angles. As she got older, Beatrix often went to the Natural History Museum. A few minutes' walk from the house, it was one of a few places she was allowed to visit without an adult. Here she would spend many happy mornings sketching the exhibits.

# First publications

**Excited by the possibility of earning some money and encouraged by her brother, in 1890 Beatrix, aged 24, sent some designs to a handful of publishers.**

## Greetings cards

'I should never have overcome my constitutional laziness but for Bertram to whom I am properly obliged,' Beatrix wrote in her journal. Using Benjamin Bouncer as a model, she created six designs for greetings cards which she sent to five publishers. One of them, Hildesheimer & Faulkner, responded immediately with a cheque for £6 and a request for more. Her first designs were published as Christmas and New Year cards in 1890; these were followed by others featuring mice and guinea-pigs.

## The Tale of Peter Rabbit

'My dear Noel, I don't know what to write to you, so I shall tell you a story about four little rabbits, whose names were Flopsy, Mopsy, Cottontail and Peter.' So begins a letter which Beatrix wrote on 4 September 1893 to a five-year-old boy called Noel, the oldest child of her last governess Annie Moore. Little did she know that it would form the basis for her most famous book, *The Tale of Peter Rabbit.*

Annie was only a few years older than Beatrix and the pair had developed a strong bond while living together at Bolton Gardens. Beatrix was distraught when in 1886 Annie announced she was leaving to get married. But she lived nearby in Bayswater, and Beatrix visited often, enjoying the company of Annie's growing family. When Beatrix went on holiday, she kept in touch, sending illustrated letters to the children.

One day it occurred to Beatrix that her letter to Noel might make a good book, so she borrowed the letter back, copied it out and then wrote and illustrated the story in an exercise book. She sent the manuscript to six publishers, but none of them were interested. Undeterred she self-published and on 16 December 1901, 250 copies of *The Tale of Peter Rabbit* were printed. The book was so successful that a further 200 copies were printed in February 1902.

Meanwhile, publishers Frederick Warne & Co had shown an interest; they would print the book if Beatrix provided colour illustrations. This she did, and in October 1902 the first commercial edition was published. It sold 50,000 copies in the following two years. Aged 36, Beatrix was now a successful author.

Left 'The Happy Pair', one of Beatrix's first greetings cards published by Hildesheimer & Faulkner in 1890

Right Beatrix Potter aged 25 with her pet Benjamin H. Bouncer photographed by her father in 1891

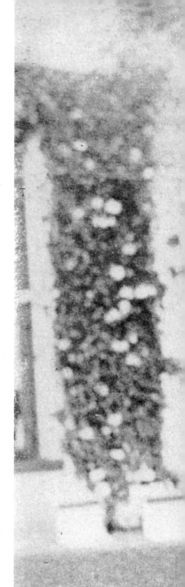

'There is something delicious about writing the first words of a story. You never quite know where it will take you.'

## The little books

*The Tale of Peter Rabbit* was the first in a series of 23 little books, all published by Warne. Many of them featured her pets – such as Peter Rabbit, Benjamin Bunny and Mrs Tiggy-Winkle – and were directly inspired by her experiences and observations. 'The earliest books,' Beatrix wrote to a friend, 'were written for real children in picture letters scribbled in pen and ink. I confess that afterwards I painted most of the little pictures to please myself.'

*Eastwood Dunkeld*
*Sep 4th 93*

*My dear Noel,*
*I don't know what to write to you, so I shall tell you a story about four little rabbits.*
*whose names were—*

*Flopsy, Mopsy, Cottontail*
*and Peter*

*They lived with their mother in a sand bank under the root of a big fir tree.*

Above This picture letter from Beatrix Potter to Noel Moore formed the basis for *The Tale of Peter Rabbit*

# Falling in love with the Lake District

**When Dalguise House was no longer available the Potters started holidaying in the Lake District. Summer after summer, Beatrix became increasingly captivated by the area.**

### Lakeland homes

Beatrix was 16 when the Potters first rented Wray Castle, an imposing mock-Gothic pile on the shores of Windermere. Over the next two decades, they stayed in a number of inspiring Lake District homes: Holehird had vast views of Windermere, Lakefield overlooked Esthwaite Water and the Coniston hills, and Lingholm – Beatrix's favourite – was situated on the shores of Derwentwater, its nearby woods teeming with red squirrels.

### Seeing Sawrey

In July 1896 the Potters first stayed at Lakefield in the village of Near Sawrey. At the age of 30 Beatrix fell in love with the village that was later to become her home. 'It is as nearly perfect a little place as I have ever lived in, and such nice old-fashioned people in the village,' she wrote in her journal of that year. She was sad when it was time to leave: 'Perhaps my most sentimental leave-taking was with Don, the great farm collie. He came up and muddied me as I was packing up Peter Rabbit at the edge of dark. I accompanied him to the stable gate, where he turned, holding it open with his side, and gravely shook hands. Afterwards, putting his paws solemnly on my shoulder, he licked my face and then went away into the farm.' Nine years later, Beatrix bought Hill Top Farm in Near Sawrey, with the royalties from her books and a small legacy from her aunt Harriet.

### Another kind of love

As her little books became regular bestsellers, Beatrix developed a friendship with her editor, Norman Warne. His admiration for her work and ongoing support gradually turned into affection. They exchanged letters almost daily and Beatrix would often visit him, both at his office and at his family home in Bedford Square. On 25 July 1905 Norman proposed. Delighted, Beatrix accepted at once despite her parents' disapproval. But a few days after their engagement Norman became ill and on 25 August, aged only 37, he died of leukaemia. Beatrix was heartbroken.

Above Beatrix and her brother Bertram at Wray Castle, photographed by their father in 1894 or 1895

Left The Potter family at Wray Castle in 1882

'It sometimes happens that the town child is more alive to the fresh beauty of the country than a child who is country born. My brother and I were born in London ... but our descent, our interest and our joy were in the north country.'

## An inspiration

Canon Hardwicke Rawnsley, vicar of Wray and staunch defender of the Lake District, was a big influence on Beatrix. When the Potters started holidaying in the Lakes, he became a close friend. At the time he was forming the Lake District Defence Society, the forerunner of the National Trust. His desire to preserve the special characteristics of Lake District life sowed a seed in the young Beatrix, whose artistic talents and botanical interests he also admired and encouraged.

# Hill Top becomes home

**'He did not live long but he fulfilled a useful happy life. I must try to make a fresh beginning next year,' Beatrix wrote to her friend Millie Warne, Norman's sister, shortly after his death. Hill Top came to symbolise this new start. It became Beatrix's sanctuary – a place where she could grieve and eventually recover.**

This 13.5-hectare (34-acre) working farm, with its 17th-century farmhouse, farm buildings and orchard, brought Beatrix lasting happiness. Although she had to remain in London for long periods of time – to discuss business with her publishers and look after her ageing and increasingly demanding parents – Beatrix made sure she went to Hill Top whenever she could. This was where she wanted to be, enveloped by the beauty of the hills and amongst its hardworking, honest people.

Beatrix enjoyed discussing practical matters with John Cannon, her farm manager at Hill Top, and started making plans for the garden, and how she could expand the farm and extend the farmhouse so that both she and the Cannons could live there. And so, despite losing the man she adored, she found the place she would love the most in the world. Beatrix became passionate about the Lake District – its countryside, its buildings, its farms and farmland – and started thinking about how she could play a part in its preservation.

Below Beatrix's unfinished sketch of Hill Top as it appeared in 1905

Right Tom Kitten, Moppet and Mittens peer through the window into Ginger and Pickles' shop

## Creative years

'If Beatrix Potter had been a poet, the eight years following the purchase of Hill Top would have been her lyric years,' wrote Margaret Lane. Beatrix produced 13 books in that period, the first of which was *The Tale of Jeremy Fisher*, published in the summer of 1906.

Hill Top and Near Sawrey provided the ideal backdrop for her stories and at least five of her little books have connections with these places. *The Tale of Jemima Puddle-Duck* is set on the farm and features Mrs Cannon and her children. *The Tale of Tom Kitten* and *The Tale of Samuel Whiskers* both feature the house and the garden at Hill Top. And in *Ginger and Pickles* and *The Pie and the Patty-Pan*, Beatrix celebrates the village. Today, you can still see the many landmarks that inspired her.

'The "Ginger and Pickle" book has been causing amusement, it has got a good many views which can be recognised in the village, which is what they [the villagers] like, they are all quite jealous of each other's houses and cats getting into a book.'

Above **The Puddle-Ducks in**
*The Tale of Tom Kitten*

# Sawrey, 'A perfect little place'

A couple of miles from the pretty town of Hawkshead, the village of Sawrey, which is made up of the two hamlets, Near and Far Sawrey, has none of the drama you might associate with Lake District countryside.

Secluded in its own valley, it is surrounded by gentle, undulating farmland and yet also enjoys faraway views: over Esthwaite Water to the Coniston hills, and further afield, to the imposing peaks of the Langdales. Clusters of picturesque white-washed cottages line the street and lanes and seem oddly familiar, until you realise you have already seen them in Beatrix's books.

Above Near Sawrey

## A walk around Near Sawrey

Heading through the village, there are a number of Beatrix Potter landmarks. Along the main road is Anvil Cottage, which appears in *The Tale of Samuel Whiskers*. It was on this spot that Samuel and Anna Maria ran up Stoney Lane and into Farmer Potatoes' farm. The character of Farmer Potatoes was based on a neighbouring farmer with whom Beatrix had many disagreements. She took her literary revenge by making all the rats in *The Tale of Samuel Whiskers* go to live in his barn.

Meadowcroft, the old village shop on the corner of Stoney Lane, is where the story of *Ginger and Pickles* takes place, and just over the road is the postbox featured in the *Peter Rabbit's Almanac* of 1929, in which he is shown sending his Valentine's card. Next door is Buckle Yeat, which the Puddle-Ducks waddle past in *The Tale of Tom Kitten*. Duchess, the sweet little dog in *The Pie and the Patty-Pan*, stands in front of this pretty cottage when she receives her invitation to tea from Ribby the cat. And the Tower Bank Arms, now run as a pub by a tenant of the National Trust, appears in *The Tale of Jemima Puddle-Duck*.

Left Samuel and Anna Maria running up Stoney Lane in *The Tale of Samuel Whiskers*

Below The Tower Bank Arms pub, as portrayed in *The Tale of Jemima Puddle-Duck*

As you pass the pub and get closer to Hill Top, Castle Cottage comes into view on your left. Beatrix bought this large white-washed farmhouse in 1909 and this is where she lived when she married local solicitor William Heelis in 1913. Why didn't they live at Hill Top? Beatrix had spent so much time making it into her own space that, rather than make William adjust to it, she created a new marital home for the couple, adding a large right-hand wing to Castle Cottage. Hill Top remained Beatrix's personal domain. Even when married and living at Castle Cottage, she would go there almost daily, walking across the field, over the road, through Tom Kitten's Gate and into the garden.

### A peaceful spot

A short uphill walk takes you to Moss Eccles Tarn, the small lake where Beatrix and William would go boating in the summer evenings. Beatrix had acquired the tarn when she bought Castle Cottage and later planted it with water lilies, which are still there today.

'William and I fished (at least I rowed) till darkness; coming down the lane about eleven. It was lovely on the tarn, not a breath of wind.'

# The Garden

Beatrix's garden provided the perfect outlet for her love of nature and her delight in simple, rustic beauty.

Although she had never really gardened before acquiring Hill Top, Beatrix had been interested in gardens from a young age. When she was just eight years old, she sketched the gardens at Dalguise, where she also liked to create little 'pretend' gardens, arranging and tending plants in small enclosures. By the age of 10, her drawings of flowers such as foxgloves, campion, narcissi and orchids, demonstrated a skill beyond her years.

As she got older Beatrix continued to be inspired by the gardens she visited, particularly her uncle's at Gwaynynog in Wales. After seeing it for the first time in 1903, she wrote in her journal: 'It was productive but not tidy, the prettiest kind of garden, where bright old-fashioned flowers grow amongst the currant bushes.' Historians have commented on its similarity to the garden Beatrix created at Hill Top.

'I wonder whether I shall do any sketching, or waste all my time gardening!'

Right The classic view of the cottage garden, as seen when you walk up the path to the house

Opposite A variety of roses grow against the trellis which edges the long border

'My garden is a case of survival of the fittest [sic] – always very full of flowers and weeds, presently it will be a sheet of self-sown snowdrops, and later on daffodils. It always seems too wet or busy at the right time for digging over – consequently, I just let plants alone until they have to be divided…'

## In the cottage style

Within a year of moving to Hill Top, Beatrix had planned and executed the layout of her small half-acre plot, and was starting to fill it with cottage garden favourites. Today it still reflects Beatrix's informal, higgledy-piggledy style of gardening and her love of old-fashioned plants such as roses, honesty, hollyhocks, saxifrage and phlox. Much like Beatrix, the garden is utterly unpretentious. Fruit bushes and vegetables grow next to herbaceous perennials and shrubs in a pleasing blend of the practical and the beautiful. Informality and the happy accidents of nature are what appealed to her most. As you walk around the garden today, this spirit is still present.

# Beatrix's creation

**When Beatrix bought Hill Top there was barely a garden to speak of – only a small kitchen garden opposite the front door separated from the house by a farm track.**

To increase the garden space, Beatrix moved the track away from the house. She added the now famous Brathay slate path that leads to the house and built a long wall to separate the garden from the Tower Bank Arms next door.

Her new garden focused on four areas: the old kitchen garden, a large paddock, a small orchard and deep, long borders either side of the new path. Walls and edgings were created using local materials, in keeping with the contemporary Arts and Crafts ethos. At the back of the border adjoining the orchard, Beatrix added a long trellis and by the summer of 1906 the beds were ready for planting.

Neighbours were more than happy to help. 'I am inundated with offers of plants,' Beatrix wrote in September 1906. When offers weren't forthcoming, she simply helped herself.

Beatrix did, however, buy some plants, mainly the bigger trees and shrubs – such as lilacs, which she loved, and rhododendrons – from a nursery in Windermere. She also increased her stock of fruit trees in the old orchard, which already featured apples, pears and plums.

## Organic growth

Over the years, the garden evolved as much by chance as by careful planning. Beatrix encouraged self-seeders, such as lady's mantle, Welsh poppies, foxgloves and columbines, to grow where they pleased. She let plants such as ferns and houseleeks appear in cracks in the walls. 'The flowers love the house, they try to come in,' she wrote in an early manuscript for *The Fairy Caravan*. 'The golden flowered St Johns wort pushes up between the flags in the porch… Houseleek grows on the window sills and ledges; wisteria climbs the wall; clematis chokes the spout's casings.' This was cottage gardening at its most liberated.

'Mrs Satterthwaite says stolen plants always grow. 'I "stole" some honesty yesterday. It was put to be burnt in a heap of garden refuse! I have had something out of nearly every garden in the village.'

in course of putting
in the apple trees !!
interesting performance
scoop
more to be had tomorrow
rain ; it does not seem
The apples on the old
a very good cookers, w

## A practical gardener

Even though she had a gardener, Beatrix was very hands-on as this little sketch of herself from one of her letters shows. In her first years at Hill Top, she became 'absorbed in gardening' and did much of the planting herself. 'I have planted Mr Dipnalls lilies most carefully, in a mixture of sand, old mortar & peat. I ought to do well with lilies, having a supply of black peat soil,' she wrote to Millie Warne in October 1906, demonstrating her new-found horticultural knowledge. Beatrix didn't shy away from physical labour, and when it got too hot, she would sometimes place a rhubarb leaf over her head as protection from the sun.

Opposite Lady's mantle (*Alchemilla mollis*) and ferns happily grow against the slate wall which divides the front of the house from the vegetable garden

Left The house is draped in sweet-smelling Chinese wisteria (*Wisteria sinensis* 'Alba') while columbines nestle below

# Restoring the garden

**When the National Trust started restoring the garden in the 1980s, though much of the general structure still existed, little remained of Beatrix's original planting.**

Period photos of the garden, Beatrix's correspondence and the illustrations in her little books were important sources of information for the team at Hill Top. Much like the garden's original creation, the restoration didn't follow a strict masterplan; it developed over time, making it all the more authentic – both in spirit and appearance.

For Pete Tasker, Hill Top's gardener for over 25 years, Rupert Potter's photos are crucial in understanding the range of plants that Beatrix grew. 'Our aim is to make the garden look as it did when Beatrix Potter lived here,' he explains. 'No plant is sourced that was not around in her time. Today about 90 per cent of the plants in the garden are historically accurate.'

If you spot the occasional weed or untidy shrub, this is because Pete is staying true to the cottage style that Beatrix embraced. This is not a show garden; it is

Above, left and right
These photographs, taken by Rupert Potter in about 1912, were used by Trust staff during the restoration of the garden

### Enlightening letters

In 1906 Beatrix wrote many letters to her close friend Millie Warne, in which she enthusiastically describes the developments in her garden.

'I have been planting hard all day – thanks to a very well meant but slightly ill timed present of saxifrage from Mrs Taylor at the corner cottage.'

'There is a quarry-man who lives on the road to the ferry who has got some most splendid phloxes, they will look nice between the laurels while the laurels are small. I shall plant lilies between the azaleas.'

'I have been very busy planting cuttings of rock plants on top of the garden wall.'

'I am in the course of putting liquid manure on the apple trees!! It is a most interesting performance with a long scoop… The apples on the old trees prove to be very good cookers, we have had some for dinner'

'I am going to get some of the wild daffodil bulbs which grow in thousands here. They grow about Windermere but there are none in my orchard.'

a homely, welcoming plot, much as it was when Beatrix tended it herself.

### Today's challenges

Rabbits are a welcome sight for visitors, but Pete – Hill Top's very own Mr McGregor – keeps a watchful eye on them, making sure damage to plants is kept to a minimum. Visitor numbers are also a challenge. To cope with the increased footfall, a second path has been created behind the long trellis.

'I went to see an old lady at Windermere, & impudently took a large basket & trowel with me... I got nice things in handfuls without any shame, amongst others a bundle of lavender slips, if they "strike" they will be enough for a lavender hedge; and another bundle of violet suckers, I am going to set some of them in the orchard. My cousin at Windermere sent a hamper of big roots, rather coarse things but they will do nicely amongst the shrubs and there were some nice things amongst them, Japanese anemones & sweet williams.'

# The garden today

**The garden reaches its floral peak between spring and late summer, but every season has something to offer.**

### The main borders

The long beds, up to 3.6 metres (12ft) deep, are filled with a pleasing mix of cottage garden plants. In spring, lady's mantle (*Achemilla mollis*) reveals its fan-shaped apple-green leaves, while irises, columbines, forget-me-nots, hardy geraniums and honesty come into flower. In summer, yellow loosestrife, soapwort (*Saponaria officinalis*), meadowsweet (*Astilbe*), acanthus, phlox and Shasta daisy (*Leucanthemum superbum*) happily mingle with roses, gooseberries, beans and wigwams of sweet peas. Autumn brings a warm show of Michaelmas daisies, Japanese anemones, rose hips and pumpkins, and the delicate seed-heads of honesty and other perennials are an attractive sight throughout the winter, particularly in the frost along with the fiery orange and red leaves of the crimson glory vine (*Vitis coignetiae*) against the pub wall.

### By the house

The red Japanese quince by the door is one of the first shrubs to bloom, shortly followed by azaleas and rhododendrons, in glorious shades of pink, yellow and orange, as well as lilacs and peonies. In spring the side of the house is clothed in the pale pink *Clematis montana* 'Elizabeth', shortly followed by the heady-scented *Wisteria sinensis* 'Alba'. A climbing rose (possibly 'Madame Isaac Pereire') with large deep pink blooms and the pale blue *Clematis* 'Perle d'Azur' take centre stage during the summer months, while the yellow-flowered

'This cottage is nearly smothered with roses, the rain has weighed them down over the porch and door.'

look over the gate. A wooden beehive sits in the bee bole, exactly as it did in Beatrix's time, and tools are arranged among the vegetables in homage to Mr McGregor.

## The orchard

In the orchard, which includes the old paddock, an old Bramley apple tree, possibly planted by Beatrix, bears fruit – a treat for both sheep and birds in late autumn and winter. Winter snowdrops are followed by wild daffodils and a glorious display of blossom in spring.

Above The garden in high summer

Right Honesty (*Lunaria annua*) seedpods in autumn

Left Azaleas in the garden in May

St John's Wort nestles up against the house. In the late summer and autumn, pink and white Japanese anemones are among the highlights.

## The vegetable garden

The lovely little green gate opposite the house looks on to the small vegetable garden. Here, despite the slight acid soil and the wet weather, four beds produce peas, potatoes, radishes, cabbages and lettuce, as well as raspberries, gooseberries and strawberries. The rhubarb patch, where Jemima Puddle-Duck famously tried to hide her eggs, is on your right as you

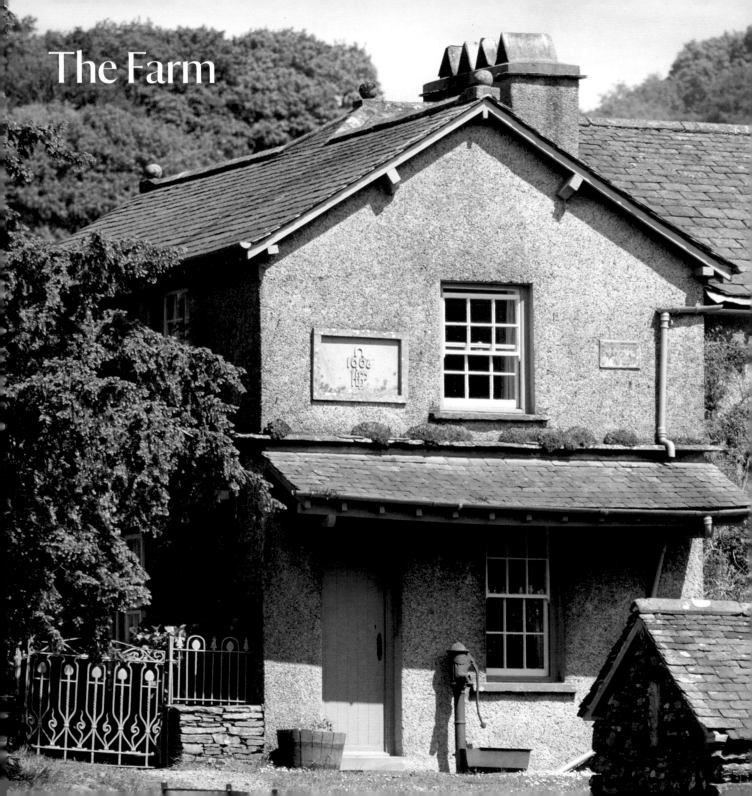

# The Farm

When Beatrix bought Hill Top in 1905, the farm was managed by John Cannon, who lived there with his wife and family. Keen for the Cannons to stay on site and for Hill Top to remain a working farm, Beatrix decided to extend her new property.

She sketched plans for a two-storey extension, and based her designs on studies of Lake District buildings. Once these were finalised she employed local craftsmen for the building work. Beatrix knew exactly what she wanted and could be a tough client: 'I had rather a row with the plumber, or perhaps I ought to say I lost my temper! The men have been very good so far; if he won't take orders from a lady, I may pack him off and get one from Kendal.'

By the end of 1906 the new wing was finished, with a plaque added above the door to mark its completion date. Rendered throughout in grey pebbledash, from the outside Hill Top looks all of one piece – a testament to Beatrix's skill as a designer and proof of her respect for vernacular Lakeland architecture.

## Learning to be a farmer

While Beatrix moved into the old farmhouse, the Cannons settled into the new wing. The farm stock increased over the following years and Beatrix enjoyed looking after the animals. She became quite fond of some of them, going as far as christening her favourites. By the summer of 1907, Hill Top had 16 Herdwicks, six cows (including a milking cow called Kitchen), pigs and poultry.

Beatrix learned quickly. Soon she was looking after sick animals and becoming an expert on Herdwicks. All this work would stand her in good stead when she acquired larger farms later in life (see pages 46–47).

## A working farm

Today Hill Top remains a working farm. Farmer Gary Dixon has been farming here for over 25 years. 'All the traditional farm buildings you see here are still in use,' he says. 'This isn't a fell farm so Herdwicks only make up a small proportion of our flock, but they prove to be the hardiest and lowest maintenance sheep.'

Left The farmhouse at Hill Top; above the door is the plaque which Beatrix had made to mark the date – 1906 – of the extension

# At Home with Beatrix

Hill Top is full of personal treasures. Every painting, piece of furniture and antique – whether inherited or bought – had symbolic or emotional meaning to Beatrix.

Idiosyncratic and quirky, comfortable and honest – this is how Beatrix liked Hill Top. Over the years it became her 'cabinet of curiosities', a giant dolls' house where she would arrange and rearrange her things as she liked. In her will Beatrix asked that Hill Top remain untenanted and furnished. Today, the authentic interiors reflect this wish.

### A diverse collection

Beatrix, a keen collector, added to Hill Top throughout her life. She mixed heirlooms with antiques – from horse brasses and doorknockers to hand-carved ivories and Staffordshire pottery. She hung her and her brother Bertram's paintings amongst lesser works by folk artists and grander pieces by Lord Leighton and children's illustrator Randolph Caldecott. To Beatrix, the value of an item lay not in its cost, but in its emotional content.

Right The view from the Bedroom to the Landing

## The perfect backdrop

Hill Top is a typical late 17th-century Lake District farmhouse. Enlarged in the 18th century, when the staircase wing was added, it was further altered in the 19th century when it acquired sash windows and a slate porch. All the rooms, apart from the New Room (see page 44), are relatively small. This creates an intimate atmosphere, further enhanced by the low lighting throughout. Beatrix compared Hill Top to an overcoat – snug and warm, it was both comfortable and comforting.

Even after she was married and living at Castle Cottage, Hill Top acted as her refuge. She would often say: 'I'm going over to keep the old house company.' Beatrix visited Hill Top almost every day. What she did here exactly, we shall never know, though she did write and paint at Hill Top. And we can be sure that, amongst the peace and quiet, she enjoyed listening to her clocks, which she described as 'the heartbeat' of the house.

'It will always remain Beatrix Potter's house and it cannot be truly hers unless a good bit of the unusual character introduced by her remains. She loved pretty things & simple things, & odd things. In Hill Top she wanted to find a home for them all.'

Ethel Hartley, who lived at
Hill Top for a year in 1944

## Objects with meaning

Beatrix's belief that objects had a symbolic value reflected the Arts & Crafts philosophy. Like William Morris, she thought that hand-crafted pieces had an honesty and charm that machine-made objects simply didn't have. She loved old Lakeland furniture, of which there are a few pieces at Hill Top, and bemoaned the fact that such pieces were being 'riven out of ancestral homes'.

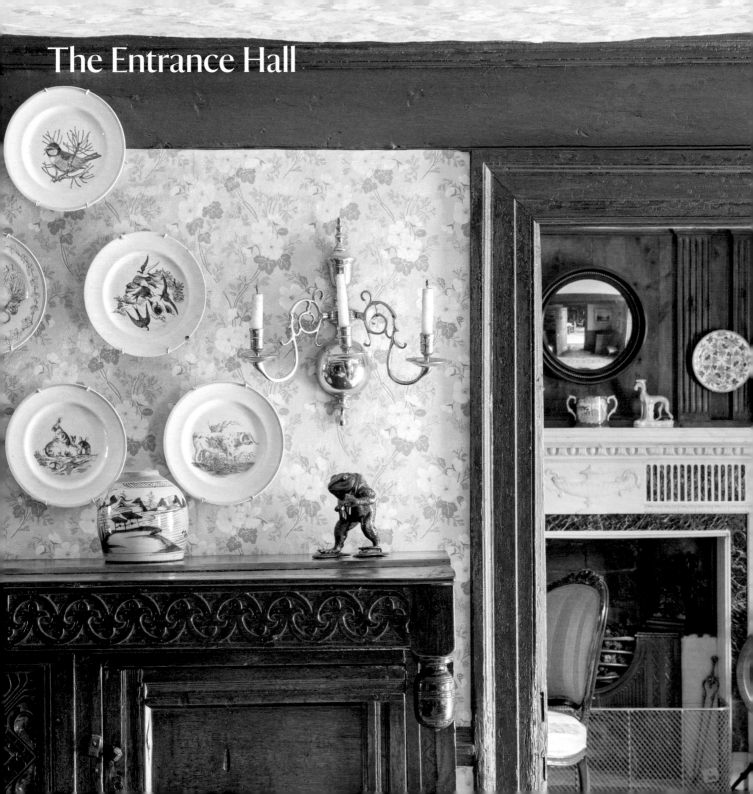

**As you walk through the front door, you are immersed in the snug atmosphere of the Entrance Hall. This was the heart of the home – Lakeland farmers referred to it as the firehouse or houseplace. Beatrix called it the Entrance Hall, clearly exposing her middle-class roots.**

## First impressions

Visitors often remark on the relative darkness of the house. During the day Beatrix would have relied on light from the windows. In the evening, she lit a single candle or an oil lamp and took it with her as required. While the low lighting creates a cosy atmosphere, it also produces interesting plays of light and shade which help draw attention to certain elements, particularly the gloss of the furniture.

Simplicity is everywhere: in the practical beauty of the stove; the rustic charm of the oak furniture, rushed-seated chairs and spinning wheel; the rugged stone-flagged floor; and the peg (or rag) rug made from scraps of waste fabric. Even the wallpaper, introduced by Beatrix soon after she bought Hill Top and which covers the walls and ceiling, is typical of farmhouse interiors.

## Key pieces

The carved oak cupboard was Beatrix's favourite piece of Lakeland furniture. Dating from 1667, she bought it at a farm auction. She drew it, and other pieces of Lakeland furniture, adding her comments to her sketches. 'It is very plain, except the middle, fixed panel, which has good carving,' she wrote. 'I have a theory,' she told an American correspondent about the motifs on Lakeland furniture, 'that the craftsmen who carved our designs were imitating the runic interlacing.' Beatrix was fascinated by old furniture and became something of an expert on the subject.

The series of plates above the cupboard display designs of birds and other animals by Beatrix's father. These hung in the nursery at Bolton Gardens and probably inspired Beatrix, at the age of 14, to have a go at transfer printing on ceramic. On the Welsh dresser against the far wall you can see the results of her experiment: two trivets with delicate depictions of rabbits.

Left The carved oak cupboard in the Entrance Hall was one of Beatrix's favourite pieces of Lakeland furniture

### In the little books

The Entrance Hall makes a number of appearances in *The Tale of Samuel Whiskers* – as do many other parts of the house. Ribby the cat stands in the doorway as she comes to borrow yeast from her cousin Tabitha. The cousins sit by the stove on the peg rug. Anna Maria the rat runs past the sideboard, stealing the dough. And Tom Kitten is shown about to jump up the chimney in the stove, as he tries to escape from his mother.

# The Parlour

Already one senses a house that is not as straightforward as it first appears. For although Beatrix claimed she wanted to preserve Hill Top as a typical Lakeland farmhouse, she inevitably – and indeed consciously – made it her own. In doing so she created something of a hybrid, mixing styles and influences.

**Originally a bedroom, the Parlour was transformed by Beatrix into a small drawing room where she would entertain guests she didn't know very well. Friends and family would be seen upstairs in the Sitting Room.**

While the Entrance Hall has rustic appeal, the Parlour is more refined. Elegant furniture blends with the wood-panelled walls and, along with the neoclassical marble chimneypiece, offer a glimpse of how Beatrix's childhood home must have looked. Other delicate touches include a rosewood writing box, a fold-over mahogany card table, 19th-century framed silhouettes, and Chinese and English porcelain in the corner cabinet.

## Country pursuits

Some of the objects in the Parlour are particularly revealing of Beatrix's interests. On the mantelpiece are two Staffordshire pottery greyhounds, each with a hare in its mouth. Hunting memorabilia was frequently to be found in farmhouses at this time and as her biographer Margaret Lane rightly pointed out: 'The pursuit and prey theme runs undisguised through many of the tales.' Despite this, Beatrix left clear instructions in her will that hunting with otter hounds was to be banned on her Troutbeck Park estate.

Beatrix's passion for farming is also evident in this room. On the bookshelves are sheep-breeding trophies and certificates, along with two photographs of Beatrix at agricultural shows. Beatrix enjoyed discussing sheep-breeding with the most rugged of farmers, breeders and stockmen. 'I am the chair at the Herdwick Breeders' Association meetings. You would laugh to see me, amongst the other farmers – usually in a tavern (!) after a sheep fair,' she wrote. She was President-elect of the Association at the time of her death.

## 'My little rabbits'

The little grass bag in the room was a gift from a girl called Louisa Ferguson, a fan of Beatrix's books. Many children sent Beatrix letters, which she treasured. She called her young readers her 'little rabbits' and her 'shilling people'. Keen that her books be accessible to all, Beatrix made sure they cost no more than a shilling.

### In the little books

The Edward VII coronation tea pot in the corner cupboard appears in the *Tale of the Pie and the Patty-Pan*.

'I shall always have a preference for cheap books myself – even if they did not pay. All my little friends happen to be shilling people. I do dislike the modern fashion of giving children heaps of expensive things which they don't look at twice.'

Opposite The mantelpiece with Beatrix's Staffordshire pottery greyhounds

Left The Parlour, with a small table set for tea; this is where Beatrix would entertain 'formal' guests

# The Staircase

**Beatrix loved the staircase at Hill Top. As you stand in the Entrance Hall, the light from the window beckons you up, inviting you to pause on the half-landing and enjoy the view towards the village.**

In the 1740s Lakeland farmers experienced a boom and many of them could afford to extend their houses. Hill Top's rather grand dog-leg staircase was added at this time, replacing a small spiral staircase in the Entrance Hall. The large window is glazed with crown glass, which distorts the light, creating watery effects on the oak floorboards, handrails and balusters.

On a simple oak stool by the window is an alabaster copy of *The Reading Girl* by 19th-century Italian sculptor Pietro Magni. Combining the rustic and the refined, these two objects are yet another reminder that this is the home of a Londoner-turned-countrywoman. Beatrix referred to the little seat as a 'coffin' stool, saying: 'Its explanation is an old custom of resting the coffin on two stools in order to be safe from rats!' It may not be a coincidence that *The Tale of Samuel Whiskers*, with its many Hill Top-inspired interiors, is about a house infested with rats.

Two oversized paintings hang almost incongruously on the staircase walls. One is by the Genoese 17th-century painter Giovanni Castiglione and entitled *Thanksgiving after the Flood*. The other is a copy of *The Hon Mrs Graham* by Thomas Gainsborough. Both paintings were originally at Bolton Gardens.

Right The half-landing

# The Landing

One of the closed doors hides a small room which Beatrix used as a dark room. Like her father, she practised photography. Another door gives on to Beatrix's bathroom, in which she would have kept a tin bath. Nearby, in the narrow corridor, yet another door gave access to the farmhouse, into which Beatrix would come and go as she pleased, to the possible irritation of the Cannon family. Here and elsewhere in the house, the multitude of doors and cupboards evokes Mrs Tabitha Twitchit's house in *The Tale of Samuel Whiskers*.

'It was an old, old house, full of cupboards and passages. Some of the walls were four feet thick, and there used to be queer noises inside them, as if there might be a little secret staircase. Certainly there were odd little jagged doorways in the wainscot…'

*The Tale of Samuel Whiskers*

**In the little books**
Tabitha Twitchit is depicted on the half-landing in *The Tale of Samuel Whiskers* as she searches for her son, Tom Kitten. Elsewhere in the book, Samuel Whiskers is shown stealing the butter at the bottom of the stairs and pushing a rolling pin across the landing ('He pushed it in front of him with his paws, like a brewer's man trundling a barrel.')

Left A copy of *The Reading Girl* by 19th-century Italian sculptor Pietro Magni

# The Bedroom

**Beatrix only occasionally slept in this room and never used the bed you see today, which she bought after moving to Castle Cottage.**

## Patterns and symbols

Acquired from a nearby farm, this fine 17th-century Lake District tester bed is decorated with attractive stylised carvings. The patterns are echoed in Beatrix's red and gold embroideries on the bed hangings, which pick out the floral shapes on the green damask.

Like many of her female contemporaries, Beatrix was an accomplished needlewoman. In the Sitting Room you can see her embroidery frame.

The quilt on the bed is of American origin, and so too is the small Windsor chair. There are other American pieces in the house, all of which originate from Belmount near Hawkshead, the home of an elderly American lady named Rebecca Owen, which Beatrix later came to own.

'I have been embroidering a valance for an old 4 poster bed. I used some old green damask and worked on it with old gold coloured silk.'

Right The Bedroom, with its unmistakable William Morris 'Daisy' pattern wallpaper

Like much Lakeland furniture, the chest features symbolic carvings designed to bestow certain blessings on the household. These would have been easily 'read' by its original owners: pomegranates represent fertility, the vines fruitfulness and the tulips opulence and wealth.

The William Morris 'Daisy' wallpaper, a very popular design, works particularly well in this room. Beatrix remarked that the daisies 'are not suitable as a background for pictures in watercolours or prints, being a decoration in themselves, but for a background to my 4 poster nothing could be better'.

Perhaps the most personal element in the bedroom is the carved wooden lintel and shelf above the fireplace. Inscribed with the letters WHB, it was added by William in 1934 to celebrate the couple's 21st wedding anniversary.

Above One of the panels on the Lakeland chest in the Bedroom

# The Treasure Room

**Filled with curios and artefacts – from pottery, porcelain and jewellery to miniatures of Beatrix's famous characters and little pictures – this room is a veritable cabinet of curiosities.**

The 19th-century ebonised cabinet houses an eclectic selection of items, some of which belonged to Beatrix's mother and grandmother. Look closely and you will see miniature bronzes of characters from her books (still available in the shop), as well as two ceramic figures, one featuring Benjamin Bunny, the other is a lady mouse from *The Tailor of Gloucester*. Also displayed here are pieces from the Potter family dinner service showing the Potter crest, items of costume jewellery, odd bits of silverware, old pottery marbles, little boxes, and delicate pieces of Wedgwood jasperware.

## Unusual pictures

On one of the walls hangs a rare early 19th-century tinsel picture. Usually depicting actors and actresses, tinsel pictures were black-and-white prints sold with stick-on metal foil, paints and fabric. By adorning the illustration with these additional elements, theatregoers could introduce some of the drama of the stage into their own homes. This picture shows a Mr Payne as Robin Hood and was published in 1839. Also in the room are some 1790s pastoral portraits and a sentimental Victorian scene, *Girls on a Jetty*, by George Dunlop Leslie RA (1835–1921).

## Influential illustrator

Randolph Caldecott (1846–1886) was a renowned Victorian illustrator, whose work Rupert Potter collected and Beatrix greatly admired. In the Treasure Room are two of his illustrations, one of which shows a woman hanging washing in an orchard. 'This pretty maid hanging out the clothes was Caldecott's maid at the house in Surrey,' wrote Beatrix. Another Caldecott painting – in oils – also hangs in the Treasure Room.

In 1902, shortly after publishing Peter Rabbit, Beatrix suggested to Norman Warne a book of nursery rhymes with illustrations in the style of Caldecott and another famous Victorian artist, Walter Crane. Clearly at this point she was not yet fully aware of her unique talent.

Left Miniature bronze characters from Beatrix's books

## In the little books

The fully furnished dolls' house contains items which appear in *The Tale of Two Bad Mice*: the food that Hunca Munca and Tom Thumb stole, the cutlery, saucepan, griddle, iron, bellows, cradle, birdcage and coal scuttle. Most of these pieces were bought from Hamley's, the London toy shop, by Norman Warne. Of his purchases, Beatrix remarked: 'The things will do beautifully; the ham's appearance is enough to cause indigestion'. Above the dolls' house is Peter Rabbit's red and white spotted handkerchief.

'It may sound odd to talk about mine & Caldecott's at the same time, but I think I could at least try to do better than Peter Rabbit, and if you do not care to risk another book I could pay for it.'

Left The doll's house features items which Beatrix used in *The Tale of Two Bad Mice*

# The Sitting Room

**Beatrix set this space out as a small sitting room for entertaining friends and family. Here, as in the Parlour, she was replicating her former London life. At Bolton Gardens, the Potters – like most middle-class Victorians – had an upstairs room for relaxed get-togethers.**

## Music and marriage

The early 19th-century mahogany piano may well have provided the entertainment, as William was very fond of music. He was also a keen country dancer, winning cups and trophies with the village team. Beatrix wrote to her cousin before marrying local solicitor William Heelis in 1913: 'He is 42 (I am 47) very quiet – dreadfully shy, but I'm sure he will be more comfortable married… He is in every way satisfactory.' Beatrix was right; theirs was a happy marriage and William blossomed.

## A troubled brother

There are a number of paintings in this room, including a coastal scene by Lord Leighton and a picture entitled *Spring* in gouache by Beatrix herself, but perhaps the most interesting is *Geese at Sunset* by Beatrix's brother, Bertram.

Bertram's art displayed all the sentimentality and love of nature one would expect from a follower of Millais, yet his oils have a darkness that reveals a tortured soul. Throughout his adult life, he was plagued by alcoholism. His sudden death of a cerebral haemorrhage at the age of 46 was a shock to Beatrix. Like her, he had escaped his London roots to become a farmer. Unlike her, he had lived a lie. In 1902, he secretly eloped to Edinburgh and married Mary Welsh Scott, whom he had met while on holiday in Scotland. For 11 years he hid his marriage from his parents, knowing they would not approve.

## 'Little side shows'

The late 18th-century mahogany bureau bookcase displays a variety of china pieces, including souvenirs and merchandise associated with the little books, including a lovely 1920s Peter Rabbit children's tea set by Grimwade.

Beatrix was a shrewd businesswoman and pioneering merchandiser. A few months after publishing *The Tale of Peter Rabbit*, she started working on a Peter Rabbit doll. She proudly wrote to Norman Warne: 'I am cutting out calico patterns of Peter, I have not got it right yet, but the expression is going to be lovely; especially the whiskers.' Soon Peter, Benjamin Bunny, Jemima Puddle-Duck and Tom Kitten were adorning all manner of spin-off items – from calendars, stationery and wallpaper to jigsaw puzzles, slippers and games. She called these her 'little side shows'.

'I married very happily… What are the words in *The Tempest*? "Spring came to you at the farthest, at the latter end of harvest."'

**In the little books**
The mirror on the chest of drawers appears in *The Tale of Tom Kitten*.

Opposite Beatrix Potter and William Heelis at Bolton Gardens in 1913, the year of their marriage

Left The Sitting Room was a place for relaxed entertainment for friends and family, hence the family piano

# The New Room

**Beatrix described this room as the library. Situated above the farmhouse kitchen and with a larger window than the other rooms, it was the perfect place for writing and drawing.**

As you walk along the narrow corridor towards the New Room and glance at the etchings by Bertram, nothing prepares you for the sight of four huge landscape paintings, also by Beatrix's brother. The canvases take up much of the wall space and create a somewhat overpowering atmosphere. With its neoclassical wood panelling, large proportions and high ceiling, this room feels as though it belongs to a different house, until you realise it is part of the 1906 extension.

## Beatrix the writer
Beatrix used the bureau bookcase in the corner of the room to write letters and to compose her little books. The elegant bentwood chair, by 19th-century German furniture maker Michael Thonet, is from Camfield Place, her grandmother Jessie's home. Beatrix wrote fondly about her childhood memories at Camfield and was certainly very attached to this piece of furniture, as it features in several of her illustrations.

Above The New Room is decorated with four large canvases by Beatrix's brother Bertram

Right The bureau bookcase where Beatrix wrote copious letters and some of her little books

## An artistic family

The New Room features works by each of Beatrix's family members, not just her brother. Tucked in a corner are three small works: one by her mother, one by her father and one by herself – a visual reminder that Beatrix was surrounded by an artistic family who always encouraged her artwork.

## Inspired by nature

Several items in this room illustrate Beatrix's love of nature, particularly her copy of Gerard's *Herbal*, published in 1633. Its botanical illustrations and descriptions of plant properties would have provided her with both inspiration and information, as did the butterfly case and the stuffed bittern by the bureau.

### In the little books

The view from the New Room window – looking up Stoney Lane towards Moss Eccles Tarn – appears in *The Tale of Samuel Whiskers*.

# Life in the Lake District

**After marrying William and settling into Castle Cottage, Beatrix became absorbed in her simple, rural life.**

Gone were the days when she published two little books a year. As Mrs Heelis, Beatrix only published six books, many of which were based on earlier work. In 1919, she wrote of her books: 'I am utterly tired of doing them, and my eyes are wearing out.' Her eyesight was indeed failing, but her love of the Lake District and her passion for farming were growing stronger.

In 1923 she bought Troutbeck Park Farm – a wild and lonely 800-hectare (2,000-acre) fell farm a few miles north of Windermere. She spent whole days there, relying on bread and cheese for sustenance and working hard in her usual well-worn attire. She liked to tell the story of how, when a tramp accosted her while she was looking after her lambs in bad weather, he exclaimed: 'It's a sad weather for the likes o' thee and me!'

But Mrs Heelis was also a powerful landlady. She eventually owned 15 farms and extensive tracts of land in the Lake District. As one of the biggest landowners in the area, she strove to help her tenants maintain a living from their farms and to protect land from development. As a caring landlady, she kept her rents low and, when winter came and there was no work on the farms, she would carry on employing her older tenants.

Above Beatrix's biggest acquisition was Troutbeck, a vast fell farm north of Windermere

Left Beatrix Potter at Keswick Show with a fellow judge, 1930s

## Working with the National Trust

In the last decades of her life, Beatrix developed a fruitful relationship with the National Trust, buying pieces of land for the organisation and managing farm property on its behalf. In 1930, she acquired the vast 1,600-hectare (4,000-acre) Monk Coniston estate (which was under threat from developers) on condition that the Trust bought half of it as soon as it was able to. She promised that the rest would come to the organisation on her death.

'Those of us who have felt the spirit of the fells reckon little of passing praise; but I do value the esteem of others who have understanding. It seems that we have done a big thing; without premeditation; suddenly; inevitably – what else could one do? It will be a happy consummation if the Trust is able to turn this quixotic venture into a splendid reality.'

Letter to John Bailey, Chairman of the National Trust, 15 February 1930, on the appeal to acquire the huge Monk Coniston Estate in the Lake District

# Beatrix's Legacy

'I would rather keep going till I drop – early or late – never mind what the work is, so long as it is useful and well done.'

**In September 1943 Beatrix contracted bronchitis. The illness affected her heart and, on the evening of 22 December 1943, she died with William at her side.**

There was to be 'no mourning, no flowers, and no letters'. Her ashes were scattered, at her request, by her favourite shepherd, Tom Storey, in a secret location above Hill Top. Beatrix left nearly everything to William for his lifetime. On his death the 15 farms, numerous cottages and over 1,600 hectares (4,000 acres) of land went to the National Trust, as did most of her manuscripts, illustrations and drawings. Meanwhile, the royalties and rights to her books went to Norman Warne's nephew, Frederick Warne Stephens.

Only after her death was the true extent of Beatrix's many-sided genius revealed. Those who loved her books felt they had lost a friend and the National Trust had lost one of its most generous and consistent benefactors. As the Secretary D. M. Matheson was to point out: 'By her own splendid example she demonstrated her understanding of the problems of preservation in the Lake District.' Today the National Trust still holds Beatrix in such high regard, it named its head office in Swindon 'Heelis' in her honour. It is in no small measure thanks to her that the Lake District remains one of the most spectacular corners of England, enjoyed by visitors from all over the world. The Trust works to continue looking after this legacy for generations to come.

Right One of the last photos of Beatrix Potter